HARMONICA ESSENTIALS

STERLING INNOVATION
New York

STERLING INNOVATION
New York

An Imprint of Sterling Publishing
387 Park Avenue South
New York, NY 10016

STERLING INNOVATION and the distinctive Sterling Innovation logo
are registered trademarks of Sterling Publishing Co., Inc.

© 2001 by Amsco Publications

This 2012 edition published by Sterling Publishing Co., Inc.,
by arrangement with Music Sales Limited.

Cover and box design: Jo Obarowski

ISBN 978-1-4027-9609-8

This book is part of the *Harmonica for Beginners* kit and is not to be sold separately.

For information about custom editions, special sales, and premium and corporate purchases,
please contact Sterling Special Sales at 800-805-5489 or specialsales@sterlingpublishing.com.

Manufactured in China

Lot #
2 4 6 8 10 9 7 5 3 1
07/12

www.sterlingpublishing.com

CONTENTS

INTRODUCTION TO HARMONICA

A Little Harmonica History

Track 1

Harmonicas are everywhere. They show up in movies about World War II ("Hey kid," says the tough Sergeant from Brooklyn, "I don't know if we're gonna get out of this alive. Play me a little tune on the harmonica. . . ."), in movies about the American Civil War ("Hey Private," says the Rebel Captain, "I'm wounded real bad. Play 'Dixie' for me to die by. . . ."), in movies about the Depression ("Hey kid," says one of the tramps gathered around the campfire. . . .), and so on. You'll find harmonicas in car factories, on chain gangs, and in the pockets of singing cowboys.

In the world of blues, pop, jazz, and rock, you will hear harmonica being played by Little Walter, Sonny Boy Williamson, Bob Dylan, Stevie Wonder, Toots Thielemans, Bruce Springsteen, and Magic Dick. You can play any kind of music on harmonica, from classical quartets to country cattle-calls; from sentimental songs around the campfire to rock-and-roll wails to a lonely blues at midnight. The harmonica is at once the easiest and the most demanding of instruments. It is the most vocal and the lightest to carry. By choosing to learn to play harp (as most professional harmonica players fondly call their instrument), you are joining a long line of players who have poured out their hearts through a little piece of tin.

Although the ancient Chinese had a type of harmonica with wooden reeds, and Mozart wrote pieces for a glass harmonica (a completely different instrument consisting of a series of tuned glasses, popular during the 1700s), the diatonic harmonica as we know it today was created in Germany in the early part of the nineteenth century. It was carried to the United States and Great Britain by the waves of immigrants leaving Germany, and by the mid-nineteenth century was played throughout the world.

The chromatic harmonica was invented in 1918. Because it contains all twelve tones of the chromatic scale, it allows you to play much more complicated music, such as jazz and classical pieces. It is also much more complicated to play. It is the simple, diatonic harmonica—which most people play—that really captured the heart and soul of the world. Over the years, in the hands of the millions of players who have played and loved it, this unassuming, basically chordal instrument has evolved into a single, shouting, crooning, growling, coaxing, wailing voice with the force of a brass band and the subtlety of a violin.

The Care and Feeding of Your Harmonica

Taking care of a harmonica is relatively simple (which probably explains why people seldom do it).

Whenever you are not playing it, keep the harmonica in its case. This is especially true if you are carrying it around in your pocket. Dust is one of the great enemies of harmonicas and yours will sound good a lot longer if you keep it clean.

Never play your harmonica directly after eating without first rinsing out your mouth; otherwise you will surely ruin your instrument (to say nothing of the risk of choking when you play a long hard draw note). We leave it to you as to what you rinse out your mouth with.

After you are through playing, slap the harmonica gently against the palm of your hand. The accepted wisdom is to tap the mouthpiece side since the reeds converge toward the reed plate at that end. Our advice is to tap it easily on both sides—if something is stuck there, you will have a better chance of dislodging it. If something is firmly stuck inside, don't be afraid to give the harp a solid shot against your palm: You cannot really hurt it this way.

Other than these main points, you need do nothing special. The harmonica is a simple instrument and requires little; only that you love it, play it, and get as good as you can on it.

Getting to Know Your Harmonica

Before you play a note, let's examine just how your harmonica works. You can see that it has ten holes, numbered 1 through 10. Each one of these holes pro duces two different pitches: one by *blowing* (exhaling) and one by *drawing* (inhaling). So, with only ten holes, you can get twenty notes covering a range of three octaves.

The harmonica is made up of two reed plates (one for blowing and one for drawing), each with ten slots of different lengths that correspond to a tone. Over these slots are the reeds, and as you blow or draw through the holes in the harmon-

ica, the air causes the reeds to vibrate. As the reed vibrates, it cuts off the air stream through the slot over and over, causing that unique, versatile harmonica sound.

To hold your harmonica, place it in your left hand, between your thumb and index finger. The harp should be parallel with these fingers, and the fingers themselves should be about a half-inch from the edge, just behind the numbers etched on the top.

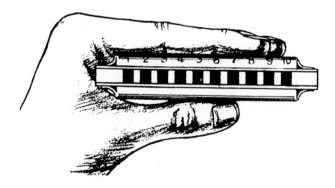

Now you're ready to play! With your teeth slightly parted, mouth and jaw relaxed, and your lips moist, cover holes 1, 2, and 3, and gently exhale. Even though we call it blowing into the harp, you should think of it more as breathing into it. When you breathe, the air comes from way down inside you, from the diaphragm. Try to imagine the way you breathe just before you fall asleep—that's breathing from the diaphragm. We will talk more about breath control as we go along because it is probably the most important aspect of playing harmonica.

Keep all this in mind as you draw in on holes 1, 2, and 3. In the beginning you will probably find that you actually have to concentrate on staying relaxed. Let your lips curl out naturally. Don't worry if you resemble a trout—that means you are doing something right! If the notes sound slightly fuzzy or distorted, it is probably because your lips are not forming an effective seal and some air is escaping over the top or underneath. Adjust the harp until you get a good seal without tensing up; tension will only make matters worse.

As you breathe in and out on 123, keep your tongue on the bottom of your mouth. You can see that moving it around changes the tone of the notes you are playing. We will bring the tongue into play later when we talk about *tonguing, bending* notes, and other special effects; but for now we want a pure, con- sistent tone. Pretend that it is time for your annual checkup and say "ah."

Chords and Tonguing

Track 3 So far we have played two chords. No matter what key harp you have, these chords are I (blow) and V (draw). (On the C harp, the I chord is C and the V chord is G.) These are the two most important chords in any song; in fact, in many songs they are the only chords. As an example, think (or better yet, get someone to sing) the melody to "Frère Jacques" while you back it up with I and V chords. The numbers below tell you which holes to play. Numbers without circles (e.g. 123) indicate blow notes and numbers with circles (e.g. ⟨123⟩) indicate draw notes.

Track 4 *"Frère Jacques"*

123	⟨123⟩	123	123	⟨123⟩	123
Frè-	re	Jacques,	frè-	re	Jacques,
123	⟨123⟩	123	123	⟨123⟩	123
Dor-	mez-	vous?	Dor-	mez-	vous?
123	⟨123⟩	123	⟨123⟩	123	
Son-	nez	les	ma-	tines,	
123	⟨123⟩	123	⟨123⟩	123	
Son-	nez	les	ma-	tines,	
123	⟨123⟩	123	123	⟨123⟩	123
Ding,	dong	ding;	ding,	dong,	ding.

Now, this may not sound like much, but it's a start! Before we start to add melodies onto our I and V chords, let's talk about *tonguing*. To tongue a note simply means to whisper the syllable "too" as you breathe into your harp. Touch the tip of your tongue to the roof of your mouth just behind your front teeth. Drop your tongue back to the floor of your mouth and exhale simultaneously into 123—that's tonguing. A lot easier to do than to explain, eh? Tongue a few chords in a row. Then try tonguing the V (draw) chord.

Play the chords to "Frère Jacques" again and tongue each syllable of the words.

Track 5 *Tonguing exercise*

too	too	too	too	too	too	too	too
123	⟨123⟩	123	123	123	⟨123⟩	123	123
Frè-	re	Jac-	ques,	frè-	re	Jac-	ques, *etc.*

HARMONICA
TECHNIQUES

Chord Melody

It's time to start playing something that sounds more like music. By playing 123 so much, you should now have a pretty good feel for how to keep your mouth fixed to play three holes at a time. As we start to move up and down the instrument, remember to keep your upper and lower lips relaxed. Keep just a little tension in the sides of your mouth where it touches the harp (not in the cheeks) to maintain the proper size opening.

The basic idea of the chord-melody style is to play three-note or two-note chords with the melody note on top. Now try "Frère Jacques" in chord-melody style, listening carefully to make sure that you are playing all the notes of each chord.

Track 6 *"Frère Jacques," chord-melody style*

234	(234)	345	234	234	(234)	345	234
Frè-	re	Jac-	ques,	frè-	re	Jac-	ques,

345	(345)	456	345	(345)	456		
Dor-	mez-	vous?	Dor-	mez-	vous?		

456	(456)	456	(345)	345	234		
Son-	nez	les	ma-	ti-	nes,		

456	(456)	456	(345)	345	234		
Son-	nez	les	ma-	ti-	nes:		

234	(12)	234	234	(12)	234		
Ding,	dong,	ding;	ding,	dong,	ding.		

Before we get down to some more tunes, practice the two chord scales below, which will take you a long way toward being able to figure out songs on your own. Once you master them, try out the chord-melody tunes on pages 32–34.

Chord scale 1

234	(234)	345	(345)	456	(456)	(567)	567
Do	re	mi	fa	so	la	ti	do

Chord scale 2

34	(34)	45	(45)	56	(56)	(67)	67
Do	re	mi	fa	so	la	ti	do

Track 7

Up to now, all we have said about holding the harp is to hold it in your left hand between thumb and forefinger. Now we are going to bring your right hand into play. (If you are left-handed, you may want to reverse these directions.)

For slow songs you will often want to add some vibrato on the sustained notes. (It goes over great around the old camp-

fire.) Let us explain what vibrato is by telling you two possible ways to do it. You'll find the second way especially useful in achieving blues effects.

Hold the harmonica as below and bring the heels and fingertips of both hands together as if you were praying to a sideways god. By opening and closing this little "tent" while playing, you change the tone of the instrument.

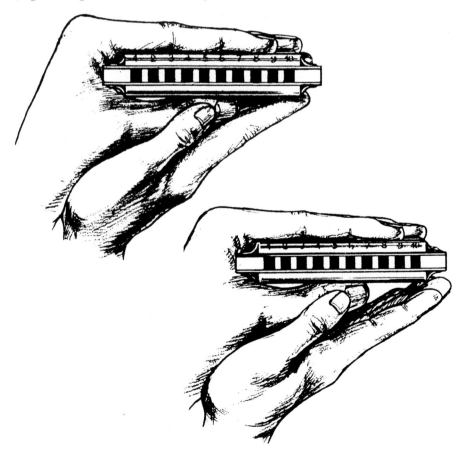

While keeping the heels of the hands together, bring the fingertips of the bottom hand around so that they curl slightly over the side of the top hand.

The vibrato effect is achieved by uncurling and curling the fingers of the right hand.

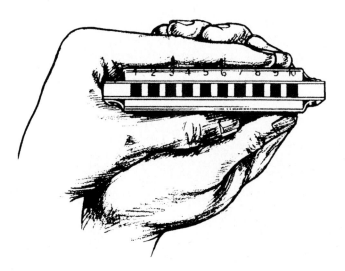

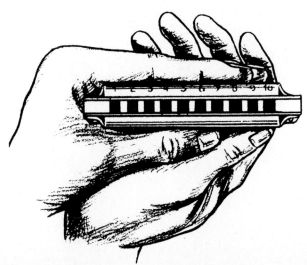

Try playing a few long chords and experimenting with different speeds of vibrato. When you have got it down, try using some on this tune: it's guaranteed to bring a tear to your eye.

Track 8 *"Drink to Me Only with Thine Eyes"*

345	345	345	(345)	(345)	456	(345)	345	(234)	345
Drink	to	me	on-	ly	with		thine	eyes	

(345)	456	234	(45)	345	(234)	234
And	I		will	pledge	with	mine;

345	345	345	(345)	(345)	456	(345)	345	(234)	345
Or	leave	a	kiss	with-	in		the	cup	

(345)	456	234	(45)	345	(234)	234
And	I'll		not	ask	for	wine.

456	456	345	456	567	456	456	345	456	456
The	thirst		that	from	the	soul		doth	rise

456	(56)	456	456	(345)	345	345	(234)
Doth	ask	a	drink		di-	vine;	

345	345	345	(345)	(345)	456	(345)	345	(234)	345
But	might	I	of	Jove's	nec-	tar		sip	

(345)	456	234	(45)	345	(234)	234
I	would		not	change	for	thine.

Single Notes

Track 9

You have probably noticed that in most of our chord-melody songs there are one or two places where the chord is not exactly right. Most of these places are not too awful-sounding, because they usually occur on unaccented notes of the melody. Sometimes, all you need to do to clean up an awkward spot is to narrow down to a two-note chord instead of playing three notes. However, there are times when, even though you are playing the right melody note on top, none of the harmony notes below will sound quite right. This happens when the chord in the backup (or the chord you are hearing in your head) is neither I nor V. It can also happen if the melody note is a blow note and the back-up chord is a draw, or vice versa.

Guitar players and piano players can play any chord they want under any given melody note, but what of the poor harp player? Are you doomed to forever play cowboy ballads and Civil War songs? Of course not! We were just getting warmed up—now we're going to start to cook.

By now you ought to be pretty good at gauging the width of your "blowhole" to play either two notes or three at a time.

Now it gets a little tougher: You are going to have to narrow down to blowing or drawing on only one hole. The principle is the same, but what makes it tricky is the increased need for accuracy. Follow this checklist as you try a nice, easy, single-note blow on the 4 hole.

- keep the upper and lower lips fully relaxed
- feel slight tension in the sides of the mouth (but not in the cheeks)
- place the tongue on the "floor" of the mouth, keeping the throat open
- breathe from the diaphragm

If you have any problems—now or ever—refer back to this checklist. Now play a single-note draw on the 4 hole. When you have a clear 4-blow and 4-draw, play the little melody below on holes 3, 4, and 5.

You can also play a major scale in single notes using the same pattern that you used for chord-melody scales, as shown on the next page.

As a matter of fact, you can go over all of the tunes that we have done so far and play them in single-note style. Just use the highest number of each chord group.

"345" melody

4	④	5	④	4	3	③	④	4

Single-note major scale

4	④	5	⑤	6	⑥	⑦	7
Do	re	mi	fa	so	la	ti	do

"Polly Wolly Doodle" is a good tune for practicing single-note tonguing. On the "polly wolly doodle" and "going to Louisiana" parts, you can double-tongue:

Instead of repeating "too-too-too-too," whisper "too-koo-too-koo" into your harp.

For more single-note tunes, check out pages 36–37.

Track 10 "Polly Wolly Doodle"

4	④	5	5	4	4	④	5	5	4
Oh	I	went	down	South	for	to	see	my	Sal,

4	5	5	5	5	⑤	⑤	5	5	④
Sing	pol-	ly-	wol-	ly	doo-	dle	all	the	day;

③	④	④	③	③	④	④	③		
My	Sal-	ly	am	a	spun-	ly	gal,		

④	6	6	6	6	⑤	⑤	④	④	4
Sing	pol-	ly-	wol-	ly	doo-	dle	all	the	day;

4	④	5	4	④	5				
Fare	thee	well,	fare	thee	well,				

4	④	5	5	⑤	5	④			
Fare	thee	well,	my	fair-	y	fay,			

③	③	④	④	④	④	③	③		
For	I'm	go-	ing	to	Loui-	sia-	na		

③	③	④	④	④	④	③	③		
For	to	see	my	Su-	sy-	an-	na		

④	6	6	6	6	⑤	⑤	④	④	4
Sing	pol-	ly-	wol-	ly	doo-	dle	all	the	day;

Musical Notation

Track 11

As we move along toward new and exciting harmonica horizons, we are going to need a more complete means of communicating musical ideas. The best way to do this is to give you the melodies in standard music notation along with the blow and draw hole numbers.

If you know how to read music, you will have no problem understanding the standard notation that follows, and you may want to skip ahead a bit.

The purpose of this section is not to teach you to read music, but rather to enable us to communicate better. In fact,

reading music on the diatonic harmonica is not all that useful since every time you pick up a different key harp the notes are going to be in a different place. As a result, few harp players are accomplished sight-readers (with the exception of chromatic players who play in all keys using a C harmonica).

Take your time with this material: just being able to read a little of the notation will help you get the feeling for the rhythm of a riff or phrase more easily. In addition, if you play another instrument, you will be able to sound out each example before attempting it on the harmonica.

Rhythm

The most important aspects that any notation system can convey are melody and rhythm. Until this point, we have relied on your knowledge of the song in order for you to get the rhythm down, because we couldn't show it using just the

blow and draw holes. Standard notation will allow us to do this. Let's look at a few examples.

In the example below, there are three kinds of notes: the *quarter note*, the *half note*, and the *whole note*.

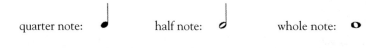

quarter note: half note: whole note:

4   5   6   ⑥   7   ⑥   6   5   4   4   4

Clefs and Time Signatures

The first thing you will see on a line of harmonica music is the curly treble clef. The treble clef tells us that the bottom line on the staff is E and the space above it F, with the rest of the notes ascending alphabetically: G (the second line) A, B, C, D, and E (the top space). When an "8" appears above the clef (as below), this means that the notes you are playing on the harmonica are actually coming out one octave (eight notes) higher than they appear on the staff.

The *time signature* (¼) at the beginning tells you that this music is in "four-four" time. This means that there are four beats to each measure and that a quarter note receives one beat. A half note receives two beats and the whole note takes up a whole measure of four beats.

Now try playing these four measures. Tap your foot in a steady rhythm as you count 1, 2, 3, 4 to yourself.

Eighth Notes

To begin playing the music that follows, you also need to know about eighth notes, triplets, rests, and ties.

Eighth notes are played twice as fast as quarter notes. Try playing the example below counting 1 & 2 & 3 & 4 &. Tap your foot in quarter-note rhythm. Play one eighth-note as you tap and the next eighth note when your foot comes up.

Triplets

Triplets are played three to the beat. Play this example carefully, making sure that all the notes are evenly spaced and that the beat remains steady.

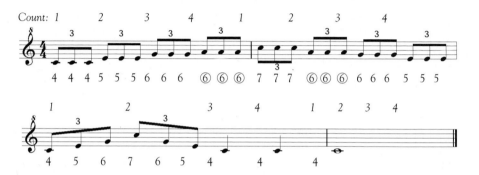

Rests

Rests indicate silence. Each note value has a corresponding rest.

Now here's a swinging version of our four-measure riff that includes rests.

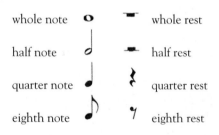

whole note	**o**	▬	whole rest
half note	♩	▬	half rest
quarter note	♩	𝄽	quarter rest
eighth note	♪	𝄾	eighth rest

Ties

We use a *tie* to tie two notes together, like the first two notes below.

The first note is played and held through the value of the note to which it is tied without any space in between. Before playing this next variation, try counting out loud and clapping the rhythm.

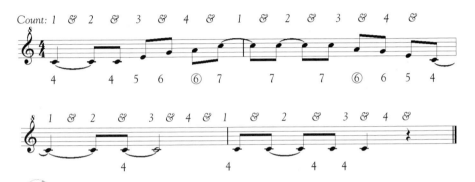

Track 12 Boogie-woogie progression

To finish up this section, here's a boogie-woogie progression that uses every thing that we have just gone over. You are on your own with the counting!

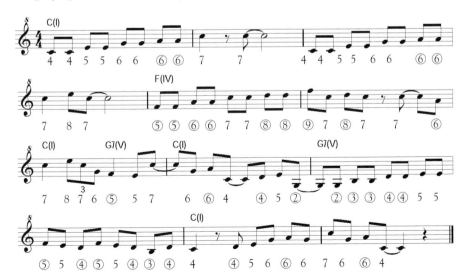

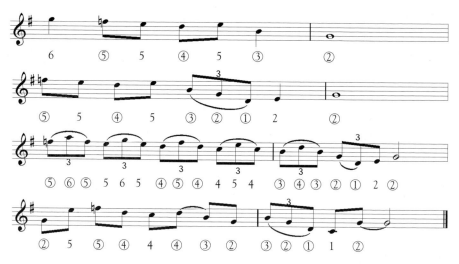

The riffs you just played all end on the cross-harp I chord. The basic twelve-bar blues progression has I, IV, and V chords arranged as shown below.

Since the blow chord is your IV chord in cross-harp playing, you know that any blow note will work on the IV. On the V chord you need to be more careful. The best thing to do is to use a riff similar to the ones you just learned that leads very definitely back to I.

Track 15 *Basic twelve-bar blues progression*

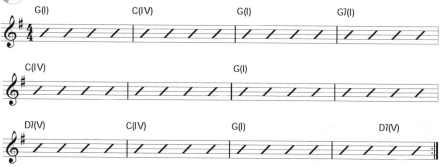

Here are two complete twelve-bar blues solos to get you off and running. Try to get some musical friend to back you up while you play them. When you have mastered these you will have a pretty good idea of how to find your way around in cross harp.

Track 16 *Blues solo 1*

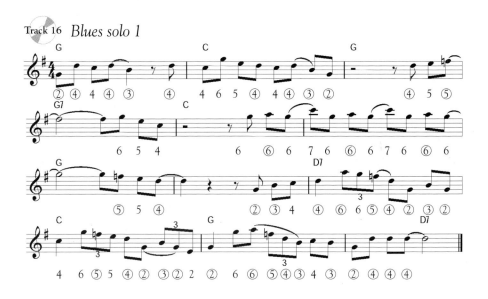

Track 17 *Blues solo 2*

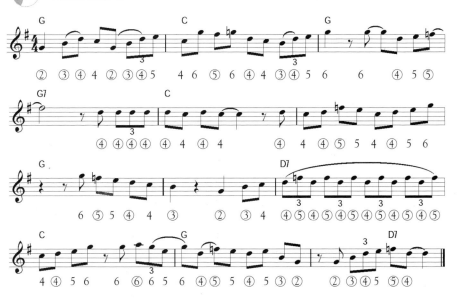

Bending Notes

When the harmonica was

Track 18 invented it was most assuredly

fixed reeds were more suited to playing
polkas, marches, dance tunes, and other
melodies that did not depend upon the
many flatted notes which are the mainstay
of the blues. It was a particular brand of
genius that discovered that the little, rigid
reeds could be made to bend and twist and
give up notes, growls, and whispers that
they did not even know they had.

It is very difficult to teach someone
to bend a note: So much of the technique depends on your experiencing the
feeling of actually doing it. In the final
analysis you will have to keep trying the
suggestions given here until a moment
comes when your ears, mouth, tongue,
and mind all unite and exclaim, "Hey,
we've got it!"

Below are a series of descriptions
designed to put you in the mood for
bending notes. Some are technical, for
the science-minded among you. Some are
more or less physical descriptions of how
your tongue, mouth, and diaphragm
react, for the would-be doctors out there.
The rest are analogies that we thought up
late at night after all else had failed.
(These last are probably the ones that
will work!)

- Technically speaking, bending a note
  has to do with distorting the way
  that a reed vibrates in the air stream.
  Normally the reed vibrates freely as

the air passes over its most flexible
part, the tip. When you narrow the
air stream, by puckering deter-
minedly and dropping your jaw
slightly (which increases the cavity
of your mouth), you also direct the
air over the thicker part of the reed.
This thicker part vibrates more slowly
and therefore sounds a lower pitch.

- Pretend that you are about to give
  someone a rather large, intense kiss.
  When we actually do kiss someone
  (on the cheek, for example), we do
  not involve our throat or diaphragm.
  Instead we just suck a little air into
  our mouth. Now picture kissing a
  porous surface: In order to keep kissing, you need to draw the air down
  into your throat and then into your
  chest, using your diaphragm to create
  the vacuum that draws the air in.

- Whistle a midrange note while
  breathing in. Now let the note slide
  down to the lowest note that you
  can whistle. Notice how your mouth
  changes: the tongue comes up in
  back, down in front; the throat
  opens up and the jaw drops.

- Pretend that you are drinking
  through a straw but that the straw
  goes directly to the bottom of your
  stomach: Suck the air in from all the
  way down there.

- Think the note lower. After all is
  said and done, this is probably the
  most powerful suggestion. If you can
  visualize it (or, more correctly, "hear"

it in your mind's ear), your body is going to figure out a way of actually accomplishing it. You can be sure that the first person to bend a note was no physics professor!

The important thing is to practice every day and to listen to master players bending notes on recordings. Don't get discouraged. Until everything falls into place, it is going to be difficult, but it gets easier all the time. In no time—if you practice hard—you might become rather bent yourself!

We suggest that you start with the ④ and ⑤ draw holes, which, in our opinion, are the easiest to bend at first. Actually, the matter of which notes are easiest to bend for you depends on several factors, among them: the type and key of harmonica you are using, how well the harp is broken in, and the actual size and shape of your mouth. Keep trying until you find one note that you can bend easily and consistently. Then try the others.

Here is a chart of which notes can be bent by overdrawing and overblowing.

hole	1	2	3	4	5	6	7	8	9	10
								D	F	Bb
blow bends							B	Eb	F#	B
blow	C	E	G	C	E	G	C	E	G	C
draw	D	G	B	D	F	A	B	D	F	A
draw bends	Db	F#	Bb	Db	E	Ab				
		F	A	C						
			Ab							
hole	1	2	3	4	5	6	7	8	9	10

Riffs for Bending Notes

The riffs that follow are similar to the last batch except that they incorporate bent notes. We will use this symbol to indicate a note that is bent: ④

On holes 2, 3, 4, 8, 9, and 10, there are more than one bent note available. To indicate how far to bend, we will put slash marks through the arrow—one for each additional bend below the first.

Track 19

Don't worry if you cannot get every note clearly in the example above. These double bends—especially on ③—require a bit of experience. In addition, your instrument must be broken in well. The more you practice bending accurately to the note you want, the more experience you get and the more broken in the reed becomes.

On the next page are basic riffs that you can use in any way you like. Take time to fool around with these riffs—change the rhythm, the tonguing and slurring, string several of them together, etc. If any particular one gives you trouble—say, with a difficult bend or a tricky rhythm—try to change it around to get a similar musical idea that is comfortable for you to play. In this way, you will be laying the foundation of your personal style. Any riff that really strikes your fancy—it could be just two or three notes in a particular order and rhythm—should be practiced over and over until it becomes part of you. All players have a handful of these that are like old friends that they can call on whenever need be. If they are distinctive and original enough, they become trademarks of the player's style.

STYLES
SONGBOOK

Chord-Melody Tunes

The tunes that follow are all written in the three-note chord style, but you can play them with two-note harmony by using only the two higher numbers. In some places two-note chords are indicated (e.g., the "old" in "My Old Kentucky Home"). This is because the actual chord for these notes is neither I nor V but IV (F in the key of C). If you are playing solo, you can add the bottom note if you like the sound, but if someone is backing you up and playing the IV chord, it will clash. You can also try playing these as single notes.

Track 21 *"Oh, My Darling Clementine"*

234	234	234	123	345	345	345	234	
In	a	cav-	ern,	in	a	can-	yon,	
234	345	456	456	(345)	345	(234)		
Ex-	ca-	va-	ting	for	a	mine,		
(234)	345	(345)	(345)	(345)	345	(234)	345	234
Lived	a	mi-	ner,	a	for-	ty-	nin-	er
234	345	(234)	(12)	(123)	(234)	234		
And	his	daugh-	ter,	Cle-	men-	tine.		

Track 22 *"My Old Kentucky Home"*

234	(234)	345	34	234				
Oh	the	sun	shines	bright				
(234)	345	(45)	45	(45)	(56)	456		
On	my	old	Ken-	tuc-	ky	home,		
(45)	345	(234)	234	234	(123)	234	(234)	
'Tis	sum-	mer,	the	folks	there	are	gay;	
345	345	345	234					
The	corn-	top's	ripe					
(234)	345	(45)	45	(45)	(56)	456		
And	the	mea-	dow's	in	the	bloom,		
234	(234)	345	345	(234)	234	345	(234)	234
While	the	birds	make	mu-	sic	all	the	day.

Track 23 *"Oh, When the Saints Go Marching In"*

234	345	(345)	456						
Oh,	when	the	saints						
234	345	(345)	456						
Go	march-	ing	in,						
234	345	(345)	456	345	234	345	(234)		
Oh,	when	the	saints	go	march-	ing	in		
345	345	(234)	234	234	345	456	456	456	(45)
Oh	Lord,	I	want	to	be	in	that	num-	ber
345	(345)	456	345	234	(234)	234			
When	the	saints	go	march-	ing	in!			

Track 24 *"The Streets of Laredo"*

456	456	③④⑤	345	③④⑤	456	③④⑤	345	②③④	234	①②③	①②
As	I	walked		out	in	the	streets	of	La-	re-	do,

①②	234	234	②③④	345	③④⑤	345	②③④	234	②③④		
As	I	walked	out	in	La-	re-	do	one	day,		

456	456	③④⑤	345	③④⑤	456
I	spied	a	young	cow-	boy

③④⑤	345	②③④	234	①②③	①②
All	wrapped	in	white	li-	nen,

①②	234	234	234	②③④	345
All	wrapped	in	white	li-	nen,

③④⑤	345	①②③	①②③	234
And	cold	as	the	Day.

Track 25 Tongue blocking is a method of getting single notes that gives you greater alacrity in skipping around the harp than the pucker method we have been using. What you do is cover four holes of the harp with your mouth opening, but then block out three of them with the tongue.

Try placing your mouth and tongue as in the pictures below. When you are comfortable and are getting a clear 8-blow, shift your tongue over to the right so that you are playing a 5-blow. It feels pretty awkward at first—some people

never get used to it—but it comes in handy on fast runs that skip notes of the scale. Tongue blocking can also help in bending notes if you block part of the hole you are bending.

There are a few special effects that employ tongue blocking. You can play your melody note on top and then provide a rhythmic chordal accompaniment below by unblocking and blocking the adjacent holes. You can play in octaves by using the *underside* of the tongue to block the holes, leaving one hole unblocked on either side of the tongue.

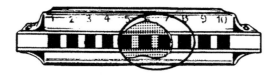

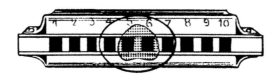

Single-Note Songs

Track 26 *"Home, Sweet Home"*

4	④	5	⑤	⑥	6	⑤	5	6	⑤	5	⑤	④	5
'Mid	the	plea-	sures	and	pa-	la-	ces		though	we	may	roam,

4	④	5	⑤	⑥	6	⑤	5	6	⑤	5	⑤	④	4
Be	it	ev-	er	so	hum-	ble,		there's	no		place	like	home.

6	7	⑦	⑥	6	5	6	⑤	5	⑤	④	5
A	charm	from	the	skies	seems	to	hal-	low		us	there,

6	7	⑦	⑥	6	5	6	⑤	5	⑤	④	4
Which,	seek	through	the	world,	is		ne'-	er	met	with	else- where

Be careful on this next one, as it goes up into the top octave (holes 7 through 10). In the top octave, the draw note of each hole is lower than the blow note—the opposite of the middle section (holes 4 through 6). Real quick—try this two-octave scale before you play the tune:

4	④	5	⑤	6	⑥	⑦	7	⑧	8	⑨	9	⑩	10
Do	re	mi	fa	so	la	ti	do	re	mi	fa	so	la	do

Track 27 *"She'll Be Comin' Round the Mountain"*

6	⑥	7	7	7	7	⑥	6	5	6	7
She'll	be	com-	in'	round	the	moun-	tain	when	she	comes,

7	⑧	8	8	8	8	9	8	⑧	7	⑧
She'll	be	com-	in'	round	the	moun-	tain	when	she	comes,

9	⑨	8	8	8	8	⑧	7			
She'll	be	com-	in'	round	the	moun-	tain,			

7	7	⑥	⑥	⑥	⑥	⑧	7			
She'll	be	com-	in'	round	the	moun-	tain,			

⑦	⑥	6	6	6	6	8	⑧	7	⑦	7
She'll	be	com-	in'	round	the	moun-	tain,	when	she	comes.

"Tenting Tonight" is another tune in the upper register and also a good one for some tasteful vibrato. By the way, if you find that you are not getting enough air while playing, or if you tend to hyperventilate on certain tunes, try breathing through your nose when necessary. Opening up those sinuses also helps your tone.

Track 28 "Tenting Tonight"

| 6 | 8 | 8 | ⑧ | 7 | 7 | ⑦ | ⑥ | 7 | 6 | |
| We're | tent- | ing | to- | night | on | the | old | camp- | ground | |

| 6 | 6 | 6 | ⑤ | ⑤ | 5 | | | | | |
| Give | us | a | song | to | cheer | | | | | |

| 6 | 8 | ⑧ | 7 | ⑦ | ⑥ | 7 | 6 | | | |
| Our | wear- | y | hearts, a | song | of | home | | | | |

| 6 | ⑦ | ⑦ | ⑥ | 6 | 7 | | | | | |
| And | friends | we | love | so | dear. | | | | | |

| 6 | 6 | 6 | 6 | 6 | 5 | 6 | ⑥ | ⑥ | ⑥ | ⑥ |
| Ma- | ny | are | the | hearts | that | are | wear- | y | to- | night, |

| 6 | 6 | ⑥ | ⑥ | 7 | 7 | ⑧ | | | | |
| Wish- | ing | for | the | war | to | cease; | | | | |

| 8 | 8 | 8 | ⑧ | 7 | 7 | ⑦ | ⑥ | ⑥ | ⑥ | 7 | 6 |
| Ma- | ny | are | the | hearts | that | are | look- | ing | for | the | right |

| 7 | 8 | 7 | 8 | ⑧ | 7 | | | | | |
| To | see | the | dawn | of | peace. | | | | | |

| 6 | 6 | 6 | 6 | ⑥ | ⑥ | ⑥ | ⑥ | | | |
| Tent- | ing | to- | night, | tent- | ing | to- | night, | | | |

| 6 | 6 | 6 | 6 | ⑥ | ⑦ | 7 | | | | |
| Tent- | ing | on | the | old | camp- | ground. | | | | |

Track 29 *"The Camptown Races"*

6	6	5	6	⑥	6	5		
Camp-	town	lad-	ies	sing	this	song:		

345	②③④	345	②③④					
Doo-	dah,	doo-	dah;					

6	6	5	6	⑥	6	5		
Camp-	town	race-	track,	five	miles	long,		

②③④	③④⑤	345	②③④	234				
Oh,	de	doo-	dah	day.				

4	4	5	6	7				
Goin'	to	run	all	night,				

⑥	⑥	7	⑥	6				
Goin'	to	run	all	day.				

6	6	5	5	6	6	⑥	6	5
Bet	my	mon-	ey	on	the	bob-	tail	nag;

④	5	⑤	5	④	④	4		
Some-	bo-	dy	bet	on	the	bay.		

Folk Harmonica

Generally speaking, folk harmonica is straight harp. The tunes that we played at the beginning of this book are good examples of the folk style. A harmonica played this way should sound like something that would not be out of place around a cozy campfire; it should remind you of the end of an episode of *The Waltons*. This is not to say that folk harp is necessarily sentimental or wimpy. It can also have the powerful honesty that players like Bob Dylan and Woody Guthrie brought to it. Listen to Woody's "Goin' Down This Long, Dusty Road" or "(If You Ain't Got the) Dough-Re-Mi" and Dylan's "Blowin' in the Wind" or "Just Like a Woman."

Folk harp can be an exacting, single-note style or a completely chordal accompaniment wash or a combination of the two. The one thing you hardly ever do in the folk style is to bend notes.

Blues harp is not one style but many. It is probably the style with the single greatest number of master practitioners past and present—not to mention the most amateurs. Players like Sonny Terry, Little Walter, Sonny Boy Williamson, Rice Miller, Big Walter Horton, Junior Wells, James Cotton, Four City Joe, and Paul Butterfield would probably all consider themselves blues-harp players, although their styles and techniques differ considerably. Sonny Boy Williamson spent most of his life in rural Arkansas and developed a country blues style that employed a lot of bending and numerous vocal and hand effects. James Cotton—one of the string of master players who got their start in the late, great Muddy Waters' band—started out a country boy, copying the style of Sonny Boy Williamson. Upon Cotton's arrival in Chicago, he found that people in the blues scene there did not approve of his down-home style. It took him years to relearn the instrument and begin playing the highly rhythmic, swinging, Chicago-style harp that his predecessor in Muddy's band, Little Walter, had made famous.

Chicago blues, and blues harp in general, favors the cross-harp position (sometimes called *second position*, straight harp being *first position*). In cross harp, you play a lot of bends but you play them in two ways: You slur down from the natural note to the bent one *or* you go directly to the bent note, a task that takes a lot of practice. Here is an exercise to help you get it down. It is based on one developed by Charlie McCoy, a country-style master who loves the blues.

Track 30

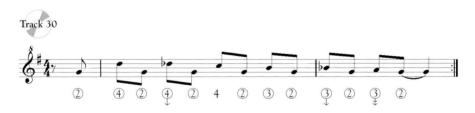

You will notice that at the end of the line of music above, there are two dots before the end of the measure. This is simply musical notation for "repeat"!

Special Effects for the Blues

Although hitting a bent note in the cross-harp blues style is not actually a special effect per se, this may be a good time to talk about some other devices which may be considered a bit more flamboyant. The first is the *head shake* or *head vibrato*. All you do is move your head (and therefore your mouth) back and forth very rapidly between two notes. Try it with the 4 and 5 holes, and you'll get the idea.

Another effect that is used often in blues playing is the *octave tremolo*. This is achieved by alternating between the note to the right and the note to the left of the tongue. To keep it under control, it is best to actually move the tongue as little as possible but rather roll it back and forth. This technique also shows up in many rock-rhythm fills.

While we are talking about single-note playing, you should know that there are a number of other positions besides straight harp (first) and cross harp (second) that are available to you if your single-note technique is clean. Junior Wells often plays in fourth position, using the 2-blow as the tonic. This gives you a minor scale (technically call the Phrygian mode) that can get real low-down mournful. Below is a complete fourth-position scale, followed by two fourth-position exercises (which will be in E minor).

You can hear that the second note of the scale is a little funky sounding. You will want to avoid it most of the time, but it can be really effective when used deliberately against the V chord.

Track 31 *Fourth-position scale*

Fourth-position exercises

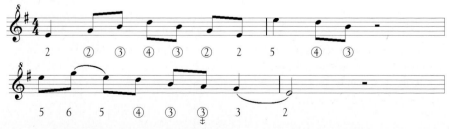

To play a blues solo, all you have to do is string a bunch of riffs together. To play a *good* blues solo, you have to do more. Start with one idea—it can be really simple—and build on it. Everything that follows must develop logically from what has come before. Learn the following solos note for note: They have been carefully thought-out to point you in the right direction. Create your own solos based on your own ideas and learn them just as studiously.

Once you have learned to walk, you can begin to run. Start improvising and let the inspiration of the moment carry you along. Keep listening to what you are playing with an objective ear and keep asking yourself if your playing makes sense. If your musical message is not clear to you, it cannot be clear to anyone else.

While keeping all this in mind, also remember that creativity cannot grow in

a vacuum. If you are not already listening to recordings of the greats, now is the time to start. If you are not sure just where to start, check the discography at the end of this book. When you hear a harp riff or solo that you really like, take time to analyze it and find out why it moves you. Copying riffs and entire solos can be a painless and extremely helpful learning experience. Even if you never use a particular note-for-note riff that you have "copped" in this manner, the practice and understanding gained will subtly enrich your playing. It is sort of like the staid classical guitarist who was heard to remark, after hearing a recording of one of Jimi Hendrix's more outlandish solos, "I wish that I were able to do that—and then I never would."

As you get into the following solo, you will notice that the basic idea is summed up in this one snazzy riff that kicks it off:

Track 32

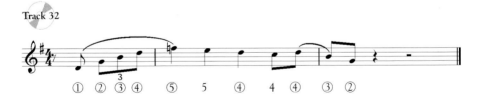

Try to identify the different parts of the riff as it comes back in bits and pieces. Notice how the same bunch of notes may be placed over the I, IV, or V chord. There may be dissonance in places, but that is part of what the blues is about.

44

Track 33 *Blues solo 3*

The following solo is of a more progressive nature. Although it works tolerably well against a standard twelve-bar blues progression, make an effort to hear the jazzier chord changes as written. There are two new techniques in this one: overblowing and hitting a bent note head-on (without bending down to it from the natural tone).

The feeling of overblowing is somewhat different from that of overdrawing. Although you must still think the note lower, your tongue and mouth behave differently. Since the blow reed is on the bottom reed plate, you must do what amounts to the opposite of what you do to bend a draw note: You must constrict the cavity of your mouth by bringing the tongue up in the middle. To go back to one of our analogies for note bending: Whistle a midrange note and then let it slide up to the highest note you can whistle. Note the action of the tongue, and make sure that the mouth keeps relaxed.

To jump directly to a bent note, you have to be fairly sure of yourself. Play a bend that is easy for you; bend it down from the natural tone a few times until you really have the feel of it down. Now try hitting it head-on. If you have trouble, try "popping" into the bent note with the back of your throat. This is sort of like swallowing, but more like saying the letter K while breathing in. The sudden rush of air pressure can help you to hit the note you want. Throat popping can also be a gutsy style of tonguing (especially useful on the low notes).

That's about it for soloing on the blues. If you can play this stuff, you can play anything. Plus you have all of those ideas of your own that you have come up with, right?

Track 34 *Blues solo 4*

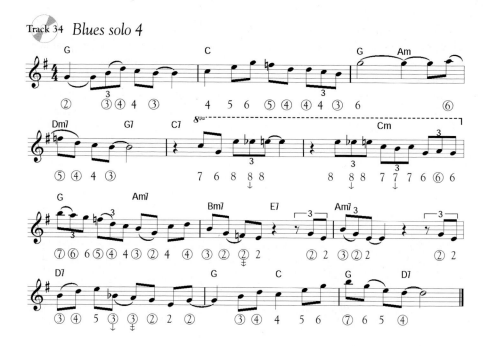

Jazz and Pop Harmonica

There are two major names here: Toots Thielemans and Stevie Wonder. Toots is the apotheosis of jazz harp. He plays chromatic harmonica exclusively, making extensive use of the keys of F-sharp, A-flat, E-flat, and F. Stevie plays mostly chromatic, but has been known to employ a diatonic harp now and then. As far as jazz is concerned, the only real way to do it is on the chromatic.

In case you have never seen a chromatic harmonica up close, here is a diagram showing the notes available.

	hole	1	2	3	4	5	6	7	8	9	10
slide	blow	C	E	G	C	C	E	G	C	C	E
out	draw	D	F	A	B	D	F	A	B	D	F
slide	blow	C♯	E♯	G♯	C♯	C♯	E♯	G♯	C♯	C♯	E♯
in	draw	D♯	F♯	A♯	B♯	D♯	F♯	A♯	B♯	D♯	F♯
	hole	1	2	3	4	5	6	7	8	9	10

You can see right away that the chromatic harmonica is a very different animal from our old pal, the diatonic. The only similarity occurs on holes 5 through 8, which correspond to holes 4 through 7 on the diatonic. The slide makes it like having two harmonicas: Leave it out and you have a C harp; push it in and you have a C-sharp harp. Each position gives you two notes (blow and draw) per hole, making a total of four notes available just standing still. To make it even more confusing, some of the notes repeat on the same hole. For instance, look at hole number 2. Slide out gives you E and F; slide in gives you E-sharp and F-sharp. Since there is only a half step between E and F, E-sharp sounds the same as F. (They are what we call *enharmonic* equivalents.)

Don't let all this technical talk scare you away from chromatic harp forever. Try to get your hands on one and just fool around for awhile. It will start to make sense quickly.

The great blues harpist Junior Wells makes interesting use of the chromatic's low bass notes by playing a C instrument in D minor (*third position*—see below). In this position you do not have to use the slide, and it is rather easy to get a mellow, minor, very bluesy sound.

There are ways to get a jazz sound out of the diatonic harmonica. The easiest way is to play in third position. Third position uses 4 as its tonic. This is another minor sounding position (technically called the Dorian mode). Below is a third-position scale and two characteristic riffs.

Track 35 *Third-position scale*

Third-position riffs

Track 36 *Third-position jazz tune*

Country Harmonica

When you talk about country-style harp, you have got to talk about Charlie McCoy. Charlie started out wanting to play exactly like Little Walter but, lucky for us, he developed his own unique style. Although his style is influenced by his Nashville location (where he plays on just about every recording session that uses harp), he has played nearly every kind of music there is, backing up artists as diverse as Roy Orbison, Perry Como, Simon and Garfunkel, and Elvis Presley. If you ever come across any of Charlie's solo albums on the Monument label, snap them up whatever the cost.

A lot of country harp playing can be characterized as coming from the "straight-harp/high-end" school. This differs dramatically from most blues playing in which you hang out down around 2, 3, and 4. The reason that country players stay above the 4 hole is that this enables them to get a pure, unadulterated major scale, which is the basis of most country-style music. Try figuring out some simple fiddle tunes like "Turkey in the Straw" or "Soldier's Joy" to see what we mean. You can get a lot of pretty little scale runs right around the 7 hole, like the first exercise below.

Also, remember all of the bends possible on holes 7, 8, 9, and 10. If you can stand the shrillness, you can get some really hip Mickey Mouse blues.

Of course, a lot of country playing is done in cross harp as well. In addition, many country-western players use somewhat exotic instruments to add different colorings. Mickey Raphael, who plays with Willie Nelson, makes extensive use of a bass harmonica. Playing very simple lines made up of sustained tones, he gives the effect of an expressive accordion. Hohner's *Echo Harp* is also sometimes heard in the background of the Nashville Sound.

Track 37 *Country riff 1*

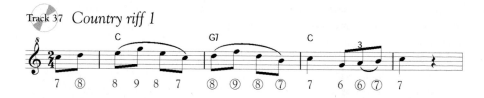

Country riff with bends

Rock Harmonica

As far as the harmonica is concerned, rock is simply an extension of the blues. That is, any blues riff could work with just about any rock song. It really comes down to a matter of taste and what you consider rock. Harp can be heard on recordings by The Beatles, The Rolling Stones, The J. Geils Band, Bruce Springsteen, Bonnie Raitt, and so on, and so on. All of them play rock, but each of them plays differently.

One thing that you might notice when you hear good rock players is that they are not coming (à la Dylan) from a folk bag. They tend to think of their harps as horns. They play simple but very effective "horn lines" on their powerfully amplified instruments. You will find it easy to pick out these rudimentary punc - tuations just by listening carefully to what the horn sections are doing on your favorite records.

For some rock styles, your standard blues riffs may be a bit too intense. Rock is, for the most part, major in tonality, while blues walks the line between major and minor. In fact, a lot of rock is played straight-harp.

One thing that goes for any kind of rock music is that it is generally played more loudly than any other kind of music. If you are going to play in a rock band, you are going to need some help to be heard. Here are few tips about the kind of sound equipment you will need.

The first link in the chain is the microphone. Some players get very particular about the type of mic that they use. This is understandable, since the quality of the mic can make or break a great sound. Beyond quality, the most important aspect of the microphone is how easy it is to hold. There is a knack to cupping the mic securely in your hands and still being able to hold on to the harp. To make it easy, you need a mic that is small and light.

As to specifics, you will want your mic to be *unidirectional* (cuts down on feedback), *dynamic* or *ribbon* type (doesn't distort when you jam your harp right up to it), and either *high impedance* (to go into an instrument amplifier) or *low impedance* (to go directly into a mixing board).

There is no specific technique that works with every mic. Just remember that the overall sound and tone color of your playing is determined by the resonant cavity of your mouth. Any mic will respond best to this if you keep it posi - tioned directly opposite your mouth as much as possible.

You will want a long mic cord to give you freedom to move around. A goo d, heavy-duty cord may seem expensive, but it is worth it. A cheap cord that shorts out after being stepped on a couple of times, or one that develops an annoying snap-crackle-pop in one of the plugs the third time you use it, is not worth a dime.

It's also a very good idea to have a spare cord on hand. Coiled cords are nice because they can't get tangled. However, if you jump around a lot, the springlike recoil can get to be a drag or, worse yet, could yank the mic our of your hands.

Now you have a mic and a cord, but you need a place to plug in. If you have a good sound system and someone trustworthy to run it, you may want to plug directly into the board. This means that you relinquish control of tone and reverb settings. It also means that the only way you can hear yourself is through the monitor speakers.

For most situations, your best bet is to have your own amplifier. This way, you can set (and reset) the tone and reverb controls the way you like them. You do not need anything really powerful: A small amp of 60 or 80 watts is adequate for most club situations; if you play larger halls, you should be putting all of the instruments through the PA anyway. Even if your amp is miked or fed into the mixing board through a direct box, having the amp on stage helps you (and the other musicians) hear what you are playing and how you sound.

Track 39 If you've gotten through the book and have arrived here at the end, congratulations! You have come from an initial interest, and perhaps love, of the instrument to actually being able to play it in a number of different styles. You have learned a little about its history and the players who have unlocked its secrets. You know how to play in different positions and keys and have an idea of the way your harp should sound when you are using it to play folk tunes, blues, jazz, and rock.

Soon you may start making your own unique contributions—find a new posi-tion, invent a new effect, figure out a run that no one thought could be played. Or maybe your association with the harmonica will remain private: You will keep it in your pocket and only pull it out to play when you are alone. . . .

Whatever you do from this point on is up to you. You have arrived at a stage when you can begin to learn easily from other players, records, and books. Remember: Have fun and do your best to give pleasure to others—that's what's playing the harmonica (and music in general) is all about.

APPENDICES

Appendix I: Choosing a Harmonica

The harmonica included with this kit is a standard beginner's diatonic harmonica in C. Once you've mastered this harmonica, you may want to explore different kinds of harmonicas, both in different keys and made out of different materials. This section will help you choose a basic diatonic harmonica that's right for you.

Chances are nine out of ten that your harmonica will be made by the Hohner company. Hohner has been the major manufacturer of harmonicas around the world for about 100 years. Despite an occasional lapse in quality control, they still make the best harp around.

This book deals with the *diatonic* harmonica. This is the most common, simplest, and least expensive type there is. This is not to say that it is limited: almost every professional blues, country, and rock player plays diatonic harp, and the music that you can coax out of one can be truly awe-inspiring.

Hohner makes many models of diatonic harmonica. We recommend choosing among these five: **Marine Band,**

Golden Melody, Blues Harp, Special Twenty, and **Old Standby.** They each have the same arrangement of notes and the same basic reed plate. The differences lie in the body construction. The Marine Band, Old Standby, and Blues Harp all have wooden bodies; the Golden Melody and Special Twenty have plastic bodies. Because of the slightly different acoustic properties of these materials and the way in which they are assembled, each of these styles sounds just a little different. Also important is that each one will feel just a little different to your mouth and hands. You can make beautiful music on any of them, and the one you choose should be the one that sounds and feels best to you.

In the comparison chart on the next page, all models mentioned have nickel-plated covers. You should try to make a decision with the help of this chart before you go to the music store, as most states have health laws that forbid trying a harmonica before you buy it.

Breaking in your harmonica

There is an old tradition that holds that the first thing you should do to a new harmonica is to dunk it in a glass of liquid for ten or twenty minutes. The recommended liquid varies from plain water to draft beer to whiskey to vodka. As much as it seems to be, this is not merely an old harpdog's tale: The liquid swells

the wooden body of the harp, making for a more airtight seal between reed plate and body. This does actually work: It can increase the volume of the harp by as much as 100 percent. In the long run, however, it actually shortens the life expectancy of the instrument by 100 percent and can turn it into a lethal weapon (at least as far as your tongue and lips are concerned): The wood eventually shrinks back to less than its original size, creating a small gap between body and reed plate that is just big enough to catch some important piece of flesh (ouch!). Our recommendation is that you take the time to break in your harmonica correctly. It will take a little longer than the baptism in beer but your harp will end up sounding

better and lasting longer, and you won't be needing stitches on your lips.

For the first few days, blow *gently*. You will find that some of the high notes will not sound too good. Avoid the temptation of *blowing* as hard as you can, but instead gradually increase the amount of air pressure. After a few hours of playing, all the notes should sound just fine.

Diatonic harmonicas

Model	Body Material	Reed Plate	Fits in Holder?	Comments
Marine Band	wood	brass	yes	the bluesman's standard ax, has a long and noble history
Old Standby	wood	brass	yes	Charlie McCoy swears by its light, flexible tone, good for country playing
Golden Melody	plastic	brass	no	a newcomer—good, airtight seal
Blues Harp	wood	brass reeds set high	yes	a good beginner's harp, but reeds have a tendency to wear out quickly
Special Twenty	plastic	brass	yes	our favorite—sweet tone, airtight, and rugged body

Appendix II: Layout of the Diatonic C

The chart below will show you which hole on the diatonic C harmonica (included in this kit) will produce what note.

Blow	C	E	G	C	E	G	C	E	G	C
Hole	1	2	3	4	5	6	7	8	9	10
Draw	D	G	B	D	F	A	B	D	F	A

Enharmonic Equivalents

Notes (and keys) can go by two different names, called *enharmonic equivalents*. Below is a table of these enharmonic equivalents. While the names on the top line are the ones more commonly heard or seen, occasionally you will hear a note or key referred to by the name on the bottom line.

B♭	B	C	D♭	E♭	E	F	F♯	A♭
A♯	C♭	B♯	C♯	D♯	F♭	E♯	G♭	G♯

Although the exercises and songs in this book are written for a C harp, no matter what kind of harmonica you have (G, B-flat, D, etc.) the set-up and sequence of notes will be the same.

The chart below will show you which harp you need to play in each key. For instance, if the song you are playing is in the key of A, you can either use an A harmonica, a D harmonica in cross-harp position, a G harmonica in third position, or an F harmonica in fourth position.

key you want to play in	harp key		
	cross harp (second position)	third position	fourth position
A	D	G	F
B♭	E♭	A♭	F♯
B	E	A	G
C	F	B♭	A♭
D♭	F♯	B	A
D	G	C	B♭
E♭	A♭	D♭	B
E	A	D	C
F	B♭	E♭	D♭
F♯	B	E	D
G	C	F	E♭
A♭	D♭	F♯	E

Discography

Below are albums by the harmonica greats. Listen to these for inspiration, or try to mimic their sound and style for practice.

Blues

Sonny Terry. *Sonny Terry: Harmonica and Vocal Solos*. Folkways FA 2035
Sonny Terry. *Midnight Special*. Fantasy F-24721
Sonny Boy Williamson (1). *Sonny Boy Williamson*. Blues Classics 3
Sonny Boy Williamson (II). *Sonny Boy Williamson (II): This Is My Story*. Chess 2CH 50027
Sonny Boy Williamson (II). *The Original Sonny Boy Williamson*. Blues Classics 9
Little Walter. *Little Walter: Boss Blues Harmonica*. Chess 2CH 60014
Little Walter. *Muddy Waters (Blues Masters Vol. III)*. Chess 2ACMB-203
Little Walter/Walter Horton. *McKinley Morgenfield a.k.a. Muddy Waters*. Chess 2CH 60006
James Cotton. *Taking Care of Business*. Capitol ST 814

Country

Charlie McCoy. *The Real McCoy*. Monument 231329
Charlie McCoy. *The World of Charlie McCoy*. Monument 18097
Norton Buffalo. *Desert Horizon*. Capitol SW-11847
Mickey Raphael. *Willie and Family—Live*. Columbia 35642

Rock

Stevie Wonder. *Fulfillingness First Finale*. Tamla T6 33251
Paul Butterfield. *Levon Helm and the RCO All-Stars*. ABCAA-1017
Bruce Springsteen. *Darkness on the Edge of Town*. Columbia JC 35318

Jazz

Toots Thielemans. *Captured Live*. Choice CRS1007

Folk

Bob Dylan. *Blonde on Blonde*. Columbia C2S 841
Bob Dylan. *Greatest Hits*. Columbia KCG 9463

These books will help get you on your
way to become a well-rounded harp
player.

Gindick, John. *The Natural Blues and Country Western Harmonica: A Beginner's Guide*. San Diego: The Cross
Harp Press, 1977.

Gindick, John. *Rock 'n' Blues Harmonica*. San Diego: The Cross Harp Press, 1982.

Glover, Tony "Harp Dog." *Blues Harp Songbook*. New York: Oak Publications, 1975.

Glover, Tony "Little Sun." *Blues Harp*. New York: Oak Publications, 1965.

Glover, Tony. *Rock Harp*. New York: Oak Publications, 1981.

Hunter, Richard. *Jazz Harp*. New York: Oak Publications, 1980.

Terry, Sonny; Cooper, Kent; and Palmer, Fred. *The Harp Styles of Sonny Terry*. New York: Oak Publications,
1975.

CD Track Listings

1. Intro
2. First Steps
3. Chords
4. "Frère Jacques"
5. Tonguing
6. Chord Melody
7. Vibrato
8. "Drink to Me Only with Thine Eyes"
9. Single Notes
10. "Polly Wolly Doodle"
11. Notation
12. Boogie-Woogie Progession
13. The Blues
14. Ten Cross-Harp Blues Riffs
15. Cross-Harp Blue Progression
16. Twelve-Bar Blues Solo #1
17. Twelve-Bar Blues Solo #2
18. Bending Notes
19. Riffs
20. Ten Riffs Using Bends
21. "Oh, My Darling Clementine"
22. "My Old Kentucky Home"
23. "Oh, When the Saints Go Marching In"
24. "The Streets of Laredo"
25. Tongue Blocking
26. "Home, Sweet Home"
27. "She'll Be Coming Around the Mountain"
28. "Tenting Tonight"
29. "The Camptown Races"
30. Blues Harmonica
31. The Phrygian Mode
32. Soloing On The Blues
33. Twelve-Bar Blues Solo #3
34. Twelve-Bar Blues Solo #4
35. Jazz and Pop Harmonica
36. Jazz Tune in Third Position
37. Country Harmonica
38. Rock Harmonica
39. Conclusion